COACH RUSSELL

Written by:

Pamela S. Uharriet

Ilustrated by:

US Illustrations

Copyright © 2023 Memoir International, LLC

All rights reserved.

No part of this book may be reproduced, distributed, or transmitted in any form; written, photocopy, recording, or by electronic or mechanical means, including information storage and retrieval systems - except in the case of brief quotations embodied in critical articles or reviews - without permission in writing from the publisher or author.

Every effort has been made to remove the numbers and likeness of athletes during the time period in which the author played. Thus, apart from the caricatures of Coach Russell and his family, any resemblance to all other persons, teachers, crowd, athletes, referees, or students depicted in this book, living or deceased, is purely coincidental.

Publisher : Memoir International, LLC

ISBN 979-8-9892942-8-2 hardback

Printed in the U.S.A

This book is dedicated to Coach Russell, his family, his friends, his colleagues, his students, and all of the athletes that he coached, assistant coached, announced at games, worked the scoreboard for, and umpired.

Therefore, fear not, little flock; do good; let earth and hell combine against you, for if ye are built upon my rock, they cannot prevail.

D&C 6:34

This is a story about one of my most favorite people:

Coach Phil Russell

He LOVED to laugh!

And he laughed A LOT!

Well, I guess that was part of his job, since he was trying to teach us how to play basketball AND be good at it.

Sometimes he would yell, "BOARDS! BOARDS!"

Which means jump up high, toward the backboard, to get the ball if the shooter misses the shot.

Sometimes he would yell, "Box out your man!"

Which means get in front of your opponent to block them, push back with your body, then get the rebound.

And sometimes he would yell, "HANDS! HANDS!"

Which means when someone throws you the ball, be sure to catch it and don't let it bounce off your hands out of bounds or, worse yet, into the other team's hands!

And oftentimes he would yell, "SHOOT THE BALL!"

Because in the game of basketball, you can only score if you are brave enough to shoot the ball and skilled enough to make it go through the hoop.

And sometimes, if we were losing the game by a lot of points, he would yell, "FULL COURT PRESS!" OR, if we were losing the game by a few points, he would yell, "HALF COURT PRESS!"

This means to put pressure on the other team WAY BEFORE they dribble the ball close to their basket.

And sometimes he would yell, "DEFENSE!"

Which means to try to PREVENT the OTHER team from making more baskets or points than your team makes.

Coach Russell used to say, "You play like you practice."

Which means if you do your best every day and play as hard as you can in practice, you'll play that same way in a game – when it really counts!

BUT..... if you goof off in practice, you won't be ready for the big game. I guess it's the same way with life.

He taught us the importance of time management and that time is of the essence! "You should NEVER WASTE TIME!"

Did you know you can win a basketball game in LESS than 1 second?

Coach Russell used to say, "If you get fouled and you have to step up to the line to make a foul shot or a free throw, you are EXPECTED to make it! After all, they hacked you all the way to the basket so you deserve a FREE throw."

And anyway, who doesn't want something FOR free! It would just be foolish to turn down an extra opportunity to make more points which, in the end, might help you WIN the big game!

He also taught us to have good sportsmanship.

If you lose the game, even though you're not happy about it, you should shake everyone's hand on the other team and tell them "Good job!" Did you know, this rule applies to every single sport on the planet, not just basketball?

Now, if you were lucky enough to play on Coach Russell's basketball team, there were a few things he was VERY STRICT ABOUT.

And, during basketball season, you could not snow ski or do anything else that might cause you to accidently get hurt. Coach said this was because we had all done so much work, he didn't want our efforts OR his to go to waste.

On game days, we had to dress up ALMOST like we were going to church! We did this out of respect for the game AND to show our schoolmates that game days were important and that we were going <u>to be and do our best</u> that day.

Coach Russell had a little boy named Matt who was 9-years old. Matt came to practice a lot so he could hang out with his Dad, but also because he loved basketball, too!

Once, we delicately asked Coach Russell why he only had one child. This didn't make any sense to us since we knew he was a great Dad. He told us that he and his wife had been trying and trying to have another child, but that maybe it wasn't meant to be.

Then one day a miracle happened. He was very excited to tell us that a new baby was on the way!

At school, several months later, Coach Russell was nowhere to be found. This was very unusual for him because he was ALWAYS at school.

I began to worry a bit, but then one of the teachers told us that he was at the hospital, waiting for the new baby to be born. So I ran to find my friend and teammate, and she drove us to the hospital - fast!

When we got to the Labor and Delivery unit, we didn't know how to reach the Coach because no one had cell phones at that time. So every time the swinging medical doors opened, we whispered very loudly, "Coach Russell! Coach Russell! Coach Russell!"

Pretty soon Coach came out to the waiting room to see us, and he laughed and laughed and said, "What are you guys doing here?" The baby had not been born yet.

We just wanted him to know THAT WE KNEW this was a very important and special day for him and his family. After all, Coach Russell was very supportive to all of us, and we wanted to show him our support, too!

We went back to school and later learned that a brand-new baby boy was born. They named him Mike, and Coach and his family were sooooooooo happy!

Now, I remember that Coach Russell used to drive back and forth to work on a red motorcycle. That way his wife could use their car.

AND he worked a lot of jobs in addition to his main job. He taught History and Sociology at our school.

He worked as an Assistant Coach on the boys football and baseball teams.

He was the announcer and worked the scoreboard for the boys football, basketball and baseball games.

Some years he was the Driver's Education teacher!

In the summers he umpired baseball games.

And he even took care of the community swimming pool at Lorin Farr Park!

But his real and most favorite job of all was coaching the Varsity Girls Basketball Team at Ogden High School! And he was <u>very</u>, <u>very</u> good at it.

Years later, he was even inducted into our state's AND our school's Sports Hall of Fame and honored as a Distinguished Coach! And they even named the new basketball gym at our school after him!

Everyone in our town knew and loved him!

"Now listen, when you get down to earth, make sure to have good follow through when you shoot the ball. Don't let it clank hard against the backboard or rim, otherwise they'll yell, Brick!"

I miss Coach Russell.

I can't wait to see him again someday.

About the Author
Pamela S. Uharriet, B.S., R.N., M.P.H. played basketball for Coach Russell at Ogden High School from 1980 to 1983. The following year, she played basketball at Snow College on a full-ride scholarship before transferring to the University of Utah to further her studies, graduating with a B.S. in Health Education. Later, she also earned degrees from Fayetteville Tech in North Carolina (RN) and University of South Florida (MPH - Global Health). She is married and has two children. Her passions include traveling, maternal-child health, and humanitarian expeditions. She currently works as a Labor and Delivery Nurse and resides in Weston, Florida. She can be reached at uharrietj@belllsouth.net.

About the Illustrator
US Illustrations is a creative, all-female agency that strives to set a new standard for children's book illustrations. They take great joy in creating compelling artwork and helping children's book authors, both beginner and advanced, to bring their stories to life. Find more about them at https://www.usillustrations.com.